BREAKING THROUGH THE KINGDOM OF DARKNESS

TESTIMONY OF DR LEONARD SOKU

DR LEORNARD SOKU

Published by

WARZONE MINISTRIES

BAATSONA- SPINTEX ROAD
P. O. BOX SR 52
ACCRA- GHANA

ISBN: 978-1-7385724-7-2

CONTENTS

INTRODUCTION

This book, BREAKING THROUGH THE KINGDOM OF DARKNESS, is Volume II, and the final part, of "Delivered from Voodoo & Witchcraft by Christ", which is my true life testimony. I want people to know that there is a reason every society believes in the existence of a supernatural being or deity. The world is full of mysteries that beat the human mind and understanding. Even in most sophisticated societies, or technologically advanced countries, mysteries occur that are beyond human comprehension.

Man, in his quest for power, protection, health, healing, fertility and prosperity, often times gets himself entangled in the webs of the powers that rule this world. The fact is that, things that our eyes cannot see are more than the things that we can see. When we read *2 Kings 6:8-23*, we see that when the king of Aram was at war with Israel, God was revealing the king's military strategies to Prophet Elisha, who in turn informed the King of Israel.

The King of Aram was enraged because he thought there was a traitor within his army who was giving out this information (2 *Kings 6:11-12*). He therefore summoned his officers and demanded of them. *"Will you not tell me which of you is on the side of the king of Israel?"*

Verse 1: *"None of us, my Lord the King,"* said one of the officers, *"but Elisha, the prophet, who is in Israel, tells the king of Israel the very words you speak in your bedroom."*

Verse 13: *"So find out where he is,"* the king ordered, *"So I can send men and capture him"*. *The report came back. He is in Dothan.*

Verse 14: *then he sent horses and chariots and a strong force there. They went by night and surrounded the city.*

Verse 15: *when the servant of the man of God got up and went out early the next morning, an army with horses and chariots had surrounded the city. "Oh, my lord, what shall we do?" the servant asked.*

Verse 16: *"Do not be afraid." the prophet answered. "Those who are with us are more than those who are with them."*

Verse 17: *And Elisha prayed, "O Lord, open his eyes so he may see." Then the Lord opened the servant's eyes and he looked and saw the hills full of horses and chariots of fire around Elisha.*

The above scripture is one which confirms that there are many more things that we do not see until God opens our eyes. This is a gift of God. When the servant's eyes were opened temporarily, he saw what he had never seen before. This only goes to confirm the fact that God's protection is around His children.

There has been a proliferation of churches in recent times. Each is claiming prowess in performing miracles. Radiant Life Christian Centre believes in Spiritual Warfare. We have been warned in *Ephesians 6:10-20*, to put on the whole Armour of God, because we are not wrestling against flesh and blood. This means that even if a human being is seeking your destruction, an evil spirit may support the person. After putting on the full armour, we carry our sword of the Holy Spirit, and that is the Word of God. Many believers neglect the sword of the warfare. How can a soldier go to battle, fully dressed in armour without his weapon?

This shows how important the Word of God is in the spiritual warfare. It is both an offensive and a defensive weapon. The scripture says: *"For lack of knowledge, my people perish"*. It is unfortunate that most prophets and pastors lack knowledge in the Word of God. They take God's Word figuratively and preach or teach their own understanding of it. They poison the minds of people with false doctrines. People get into bondage and enslavement by following the teachings of such as these. People get confused and get deceived. Then, there are also the prosperity gospel preachers. Naturally, because everyone wants to prosper, people flock into these churches and are deceived. People are easily deceived by those they consider dear to themselves.

I base my call on teaching the Word of God and on Spiritual Warfare. We thank God for miracles and prosperity preachers; we also thank God for loud gospel music, drumming, dancing and shouting. We thank God for the strange tongues we speak but, my dear reader, all these things do not move the devil. He is not shaken by your church name; he is only shaken by the power of God through the name of Jesus Christ. He only flees when you release the Sword of God, that is, the Word of God, at him appropriately.

What I am trying to say is study the sound doctrines from the Bible and it will help you overcome your spiritual enemy. Finally, in *Ephesians 6:18*, Paul wrote,

"And pray in the spirit on all occasions, with all kinds of

prayers and requests. With this in mind, be alert and always keep on praying for all the saints. Pray also for me, that whenever I open my mouth, words may be given me so that I will fearlessly make known the mystery of the gospel for which I am an ambassador in chains. Pray that I may declare it fearlessly, as I should."

This also means that in spiritual warfare, prayer is very necessary for us on the battleground. But instead of learning to pray ourselves, we call on prophets, pastors and evangelists to pray for us. We need their prayers at times, but not always. They also need our prayers as Apostle Paul wrote in his letter to the Corinthian Church.

You can overcome your spiritual and physical enemies through the correct use of the Armour of God, the Sword of the Spirit and Prayer. AMEN!

CHAPTER 1
MY ENCOUNTER WITH THE ENEMY IN SPIRITUAL WARFARE

"That which we have seen and heard we declare to you, that you may have fellowship with us, and our fellowship is with the Father and with His Son Jesus Christ, and these things write we unto you that your joy may be full." **1 John 1:2-4**.

Through my encounter with the two spiritual worlds, I know that the Almighty God is alive and I believe also in the Comforter, who is the Holy Spirit. I am proud that I am a Christian. We have to trust in God, study his word and obey the word in order to live a victorious Christian life. The problem Christians have today is that some of us either go to church with hymn books but without Bibles, or we are only Sunday churchgoers. Some people are only expecting an honourable burial and memorial service when they die. People are not prepared to have a victorious life.

Some people are old-fashioned Christians. We want to belong to a church where we would conform to the standards of this world; we have a form of godliness without the power thereof. Remember that when David wanted to fight Goliath, Saul did not buy the idea; he rejected the idea of a small boy fighting with an old warrior and a champion such as Goliath. David however told Saul that he could fight Goliath. The fact was that although David was a small boy, he had the anointing that could break the yoke of the enemy and was also a part of the covenant between God and Abraham.

There were old warriors on both sides, in the Philistine and the Israelite camps, but the young boy won the battle because the Lord fought for him. In the body of Christ today, there are old warriors with Goliath's amour on, but without the power, help and protection of God, we are slaves to sin instead of being slaves to righteousness (*1 Sam. 17:32-33*). Then David said to Saul,

"Let no man's heart fail because of him; your servant will go and fight with this Philistine." **Verse 33**: *"Saul said to David, 'You are not able to go against this Philistine to fight with him, for you are but a youth and he a man of war from his youth."'*

David shared his testimony to assure Saul that the God that he served is able to change impossibilities into possibilities. He is the "I AM THAT I AM". God gave the enemy into the hands of David. That is the God we are serving today. If you know Him and obey Him, then your enemies are in your hands.

VICTORY THROUGH CHRIST

The scripture says:

*And they overcame him by the blood of the lamb and by the word of their testimony (**Rev. 12:11**).*

The above scripture means that one of the weapons of spiritual warfare is the Christian's testimony that glorifies God. Remember that the moment you start sharing testimonies, you have started provoking the enemy and he launches more offensive weapons at you. But be not discouraged and fear not for God is with you. *Isaiah 34:2* says, *"When you pass through the waters, I will be with you"*.

In this book, I shall be sharing some miracles that I have seen the Lord perform. I want to share these things, first, to the glory of God, and secondly, to encourage others to have renewed minds about the Christian life. I just want to boast in what the Lord is doing because *1 Cor. 1:26-31* says, *"For you see your calling, brethren that not many wise men after the flesh, not many mighty, nor many nobles are called. But God has chosen the foolish things of the world to put to shame the wise, and God has chosen the weak things of the world to put to shame the things which are mighty.''*

"God has chosen the base (insignificant or lowly*) things of the world and things which are despised, to bring to nothing the things that are: that no flesh should glory* (boast*) in his presence, but of him you are in Christ Jesus, who became for us wisdom from God and righteousness, and sanctification, and redemption: that, as it is written, 'He who glorifies* (boasts*) let him glorify in the Lord."* (*1 Cor. 1:31*).

I think it is high time Christians had a united front and put off denominational barriers, man-made doctrines and in some cases, unnecessary spiritual rituals that make the Word of God ineffective. We should seek knowledge from Jehovah, Jesus Christ of Nazareth and the Holy Spirit, so that we would be well equipped for the spiritual warfare. I think the time has come for us to use the sanctuaries as

God's Military Academy and move out and set the captives free.

The bulk of the work of God is outside the chapel. We need to hold the enemy by its beard and put him where he belongs and set the captives free. A church that does not set the captives free needs to put its house in order. Do not be surprised that many churches have rather kept people in bondage and spiritual poverty.

The success of a ministry is not the number of noses and nickels we count on Sunday, neither is it the expensive building complex that is commissioned. It is the number of the chosen in the congregation, that is, those who have their linen washed in the blood of the LAMB - that shows the success of a ministry. God is fed up with counterfeit Christians. Let us plan new strategies against the enemy by being obedient to God. I hope this book, which is the second part of my testimony in "Delivered from Voodoo & Witchcraft by Christ", will strengthen you in the service of the Lord.

AFTER GRADUATING FROM A SATANIC SCHOOL

In *Delivered from Voodoo & Witchcraft by Christ*, I shared how we went to a school of Satan, and a few of the lessons we had. When we completed this school, the "principal", who was a chief wizard from the Republic of Benin, told us that we should go to a mountain in Benin. Satan would open the mountain and we would enter a new world, where plants would teach us their uses in a language each one would understand. Thereafter, we could become top herbalists. That was good news to us; however, there was one condition to be fulfilled. The condition was that one of us would not come back because the plants would keep one of us as payment for their tuition fee. No one was willing to be sacrificed and as a result, we all refused to go.

However, we were shown one particular plant that could perform anything evil that one would tell it to do. All one has to do is to wake up at dawn and without talking to any human being, go stark naked to the plant and tell it whatever one wanted it to do. Most of the time, God protects some people against the potency or the power of that plant. Unfortunately for the user, it does not bring blessings; it only answers requests that tend to destroy other people.

The Devil Knows the Scriptures

Do not be surprised to learn that the Bible is studied by Satanists. We studied the word and used it as a weapon against Christians in our demonic school. You must know your enemy's weapons in order to fight him. During the great temptation, the devil also quoted the scripture (*Ps. 91:11-12; Matt. 4:6*).

The devil went further to provide ritual keys to the Psalms in the Sixth and Seventh Books of Moses. Most occult materials and books are mingled with the scripture to confuse people. Before I became a born again Christian, I laid hands on the Sixth and Seventh Books of Moses and Napoleon's Book of Fate. In the latter book, we studied a lot on occult practices e.g. palm reading, reading the stars, divination, etc.

Since I became born-again, I have prayed for deliverance for some people who belonged to secret societies. Some surrendered books and literature, including the Eighth, Ninth and Tenth Books of Moses. *I thank God that Jesus is Lord.*

A Christian and a Satanist

Readers might think that at that time I was not a Christian.

I was a "Christian" and a fetish worshipper at the same time. In fact I was a communicant, and partook in all the sacraments and rituals of the church. There are many things I do not want to share with people for this may create the impression of condemnation of a church.

Let me share with you a few of the things that I did as a "Christian" before I was saved and became a born again Christian.

1.   I joined the Scripture Union (SU) in Ada Training College in 1965. The S.U. then was like any other church, we prayed, read the Bible, sung songs and preached against sin, but there was no Pentecostal experience. I took part in seminars and conventions. In fact, the Holy Spirit was not much spoken of. I attended many camp meetings but I was still an idol worshipper.

2.   I was the best student in Bible Knowledge while at

Ada Training College, between 1965 and1969. I won a prize in Bible Knowledge in my final year at the Training College and received a credit in the O Level General Certificate of Education, i.e. London GCE, but the scripture was then mere literature to me.

3.   I was active in Sunday services; I was a communicant but I actively participated in the sinful pleasures of this world with some of my friends and priests of the church. I pray that the Lord will transform those friends also to know the Lord Jesus as their Lord and Saviour.

God is causing a new thing to happen. Many people are becoming saved. The devil is angry. Even though the "world" has entered the church today, immorality and other vices have become more rampant in the church today, more than before, but we must move forward to overcome the devil, for we are in a warzone. When you fall, stand up and move on towards heaven's gate. God says, "When I hold, who can deliver from my hand?" No devil can snatch us from God's hand.

Is the Devil Wiser Than Man?

God created man in His image but, sometimes, man allows the devil to steal his wisdom.

I was, at one time, fooled by the devil. He blinded me and brought me below the level of an animal. During the school of Satan, I drank concoctions made of raw snails in mashed green herbs with other creatures such as lizards, chameleons and scorpions, and animals' blood. I drank this to receive power from the devil. After this ritual, I was forbidden to eat meat of antelope, taste the small wild African pepper, and many other things. The concoction, which cats and dogs would reject, is what intelligent people are made to drink in their quest for power.

Can you believe this? People are made to keep objects in their offices, homes, farms, etc. to protect them. They worship creatures instead of worshipping the Creator. It is sad that I was really lost; I was indeed a fool. The Bible says it is only a fool who worships carved wood and graven images. I used to recite magical incantations while taking my bath. I talked to myself as though I was mad. People still use protective spiritual soap and even walk naked seven times around their houses or bath in the centre of their houses at midnight. This will not help. Jesus alone is able to save.

The Devil's Gifts

Before I became a committed Christian, I was proud and haughty. I thought I was a big man in Satanic powers; I thought my blessings were from the gods. I had no respect for people. My heart and thoughts were evil. Because I had studied metaphysics and telepathy, I was able to read people's minds at will. For example, when a vehicle passed by and I sent mental vibrations after it, whatever I thought about the vehicle would happen. I used mental powers to control the physical. Believe me, I was quiet and friendly, but I was the agent of Satan.

*People travel long distances looking for gods to worship. The Bible says, "**God is with us**". Some Christians continue to obey the rules or laws of the devil. For instance, they are forbidden to eat some kinds of food and from doing certain things. They fear that when they do those things, they will die.*

I was one of such people. Thank God, today, I am free. Now I eat catfish, I eat the meat of antelope, whistle in the night, and eat meals prepared by a woman who is in her menstrual period. I was forbidden to eat all these when I was in Satan's kingdom. It is time we Christians also frightened the devil.

The Nigerian Experience

Some of us became born again the hard way, like Paul. Paul acknowledged Jesus only after he had become blind (*Acts Chapter 9*).

I worked in Nigeria for eight and a half years. Between May and September, 1978, I worked as a labourer in a firm in Kaduna State and later, as a carpenter in Jos. I got my first real job as a teacher in Midland Commercial College, Jos. The proprietor exploited us so much that I left. Later on, I got a job with Plateau State Government where I was sent to Government College, Pankshin, as a tutor. I rose to the position of Head of Department, and later became a co-opted inspector of Business Education Subjects in Plateau State, in Second Cycle Institutions. I got part-time jobs with the School of Health Technology, Government Secondary School and Federal College of Education, all in Pankshin. I joined the Rotary Club of Pankshin as a chartered member at a very tender age. I was really enjoying myself with the world, since I was getting a lot of money. Indeed, I changed my car every two years.

ENCOUNTER WITH CHRIST

I returned to Ghana in August, 1985, and got back into the Ghana Education Service in November, 1986, as a tutor at Oda Secondary School. I believe this was all in the divine plan of God for me, for the very week that I resumed work, I gave my life to Christ. It all happened when I attended a Full Gospel Business Men's Fellowship International (FGBMI) meeting and the Holy Spirit convicted me. I gave myself to Jesus Christ as my Lord and personal saviour. I was baptized into the Holy Spirit and since then, my life has never been the same.

I joined the local Assemblies of God church in the town and learnt from the pastor and the Sunday School teachers. Every evening, we had fellowship from which I received sound teachings, which built my foundations in Christ. Today, I feel very grateful to God, who enabled me to go through these teachings and reformation. Eventually, I had my water baptism in River Birim in Akim Oda. An Assemblies of God pastor, Rev William Owusu Sarfo, performed this great event of my life.

The Price of Deliverance

From then on, the devil got angry with me. He planned several times to kill me. Evil spirits appeared to me several times in my dreams and visions. On many occasions, they threatened me with death. I had daily nightmares. Indeed, this was the price I was to pay for deliverance from the devil's camp. It was a daily warfare; from November, 1986 to June, 1987, I fell sick several times and was rushed to the Oda hospital. I was admitted on many occasions and I developed an abscess as a result of the injections that I received, but I became more committed to the Lord in these trials.

Eventually, the Lord miraculously healed me. I served the Lord with zeal. I became one of the patrons of the Scripture Union and member of the Staff of Christian Fellowship on campus. I also became the Prayer and Counselling Director of the Full Gospel Businessmen's

Fellowship International, Akim Oda Chapter, and a major speaker at Full Gospel meetings. Now, I belong to the City Chapter in Accra.

The Lord Anoints Me

After my baptism in the Holy Spirit, I devoted more time to fasting, prayer, studying the word and obeying the Lord. One day, we had an all-night prayer meeting with fasting in the Local Assemblies of God church. While travailing in prayer, the Holy Spirit, in the form of a dove, visited us and anointed us with power. A member of the group clearly saw this in a vision. The dove perched on each person's head and released power. A few days later, when I am going to bed, I prayed the following:

"Lord Jesus Christ, I know you are real. You have delivered me from satanic powers; you have baptized me into the Holy Spirit. I want you to anoint me tonight if you want me to do your work."

While in bed, about midnight, the Lord visited me and anointed me and told me to receive power. I wanted to shout but all I could say was "Thank you Jesus", repeatedly after He anointed my hand. He anointed my forehead also. When it was all over, I looked at my watch and it was about midnight. I was alone in the flat so I got frightened. I knelt down and thanked the Lord. All this happened in Oda Secondary School where I was teaching.

THE CALL BY THE LORD INTO FULL TIME MINISTRY

By God's grace, I was called into ministry as a Rural Evangelist in June 1987, in a very memorable way. One day, as I was pondering over the word of God, the Lord spoke to my heart that He wanted me to do His work. I rejected the thought and rebuked the devil. How could I give up my job to become a preacher? Before my new birth, I disliked preachers. I felt they were dropouts, frustrated and poor people, who lived by the history book of Israel. But after my new birth, I felt a strong urge to move. One day, a voice said to me:

1.   "Go and write post-dated cheques for six months based on your monthly salary and give them to your pastor as your tithes."

2.   "Let your pastor pray with you and send you out as an evangelist."

3.   "When you go out, signs will follow you, but give all the glory to God."

4.   "I will protect you, empower you, prepare you and provide for you."

5.   "Tell your pastor to get anointed people to lay hands on you."

The instructions sounded unbelievable, but I obeyed them.

I sent post-dated cheques to the pastor, Rev William Owusu Sarfo. My going to his house at that particular moment also turned out to be a miracle because when I reached there with the cheques, some other pastors were visiting him. They included Rev. Dr. Harry of North Kaneshie Assemblies of God Church, Accra-Ghana. When I told them my story, they did not hesitate to lay hands on me to pray with me. This happened in the pastor's living room.

The Holy Ghost Fire

I continued studying the Bible, fasting, and praying. Often we met and studied the Bible, and prayed as a group. This strengthened me greatly in the Lord as I learnt a lot from these meetings. I felt I was getting myself ready for the work that the Lord had for me to do.

One day, we were praying in a sister's house when I saw a vision. In the vision was a mountain, with a beautiful fire burning on top. The Lord told me that it was the Holy Ghost Fire. From then on, the Lord started using me in a powerful miracle ministry. I humbled myself and learnt from my seniors in the ministry.

The Lord Opened the Door

During a week of fasting and prayer, I received an invitation from the Full Gospel Businessmen's Fellowship International President from Dunkwa-on-Offin, for a gospel crusade. I asked, "God, what can I preach? I know the Bible as a literature book." The Lord said:

"Pray; ask the Holy Spirit to give you divine understanding and exposition of the Word of God. Remember, I said I would prepare you."

That was June, 1987. I therefore went out into the evangelistic field as a guest of the Full Gospel Businessmen's Fellowship International. My first crusade was in Dunkwa-on-Offin. The Lord caused a great revival and many souls were healed, saved and baptised into the Holy Spirit. At that time, it was believed that witches in the town were using a tree in the town as a slaughterhouse for killing human beings, especially children. The tree was close to the Dunkwa hospital and there had been confessions of some witches to the effect that this was true.

During the crusade, I asked the congregation to stretch

their hands towards the tree and throw spiritual bombs at it. The congregation obeyed and a powerful prayer was said against the tree. After the revival, the District Secretary gave orders that the tree be cut down. It was therefore cut down. Hitherto, everyone had feared to destroy that tree and after that, death of children ceased. During the crusade, we had a mighty move of God with salvation, signs, and wonders. At the end of the programme, the love offering and gifts amounted to my annual salary as a college teacher. I sent the money to my bankers and sent a message to my pastor to cash the cheques for my tithes.

Our God is good. Your tithes are the key to heaven's bank of supernatural and financial blessings.

By these miracles, the Lord led me into the Rural Evangelism Ministry. I went through many towns and villages preaching the good news, healing the sick, and casting out demons in the name of Jesus Christ.

CHAPTER 2
DIFFICULT ENCOUNTERS

To humble and discipline me, the Lord treated me like Paul. I went through forests and grasslands. I was on wooden trucks, tipper trucks and wooden vehicles to the remotest parts of Ghana, doing evangelism. The devil got angry at my involvement in the ministry. I would be so frustrated at times that I would decide to quit. Sometimes, even getting one meal a day to eat was difficult.

For four years, I worked in the rural areas of Ghana with support from only God through a Christian Family. I object poverty but the Christian life is not rosy all the time. There are ups and downs, but the difference is that the Lord is with us.

Please, never give up in life. Your miracle is on the way. Trust in God.

THE DEVIL TOLD ME TO QUIT

It was during the main rainy season and I was travelling from a town called Samreboi after a revival meeting there, to another town for another meeting. We were on a wooden truck. The road was muddy and almost impassable. Some sections of the road were flooded. Our big truck would move for about one hundred metres and we would come down to push it because it would get stuck in the mud. We removed our shoes and sandals to be able to wade through the muddy waters ourselves. It took us a whole day to travel a distance of only fifty miles. We were tired, frustrated and hungry.

It was in this condition that, as we sat on the truck, the devil spoke to me, asking me a few questions.

1. *"Do you really say you are born again?"*
2. *"Where are your school mates who are not born again?"*

"They are bursars, auditors, bankers and educationists."
I answered, *"Good."*
"What then are you doing in this truck in this deep forest? Don't you think you are stupid? If you continue spreading the gospel in this poverty, when will you make it? Why don't you quit now and go for a job in the bank as you have been promised? You are a failure. You are finished. I am sorry for you. What will a small offering do for you in a month? Don't you see that even in some towns, you do not receive offering for transportation?"

At the end of this message, I got really shattered in my mind. I had a blackout; no hope. I agreed with the devil. I saw a dark gloomy future ahead of me. It was like the case of Elijah in the Bible. I had no place to lay my head. I had no fixed address. I decided that after the revival meeting in Prestea, I would go down to Accra and look for a job with a bank.

After the meeting in Prestea, I was preparing to leave for Accra. I was going to run away from God's presence. But God knew my thoughts and knew that the devil was trying to deceive me. He, the Lord, has marked me out to work, just like Paul, so He stepped in in a miraculous way. It was 4:40am when, after I had made up my mind to quit, the pastor of a local Assemblies of God Church and his wife called on me in Grace Villa Hotel where I was lodging. That was an unusual visit because I was not expecting them.

Their mission was that they had brought a message to me from God. They said as they were praying at dawn that day, God spoke to them to come and tell me not to quit the work that He has given me. I was surprised, since I had not shared my decision to quit with anybody. They presented me with an envelope in which there was a handkerchief as a remembrance of God's message to me.

EARLY ATTEMPTS BY THE DEVIL TO KILL ME

The devil is a killer and a destroyer. If one is not committed to God, the devil may destroy one's life. He is roaming around like a lion, looking for whom to destroy. One thing I know is that I have Jesus in me, and I am wearing Jesus Christ so the devil cannot kill me. He cannot kill Jesus. Two thousand years ago, the Lord Jesus Christ disarmed the devil. *The devil is a toothless and clawless enemy. Amen.*

By the grace of God, I got a car, which I sometimes

used as a taxi to supplement my income. The devil wanted to use this opportunity to destroy me but the Lord saved me in a miraculous way. One day, I had a dream in which someone presented three accident victims to me. They were dead. I refused to accept them. In the morning, I prayed seriously, rebuking the spirit of accident and death.

One Sunday, around 5:30pm, I had some passengers who were more than I could take but I decided to take them and consequently, overloaded the car. Instead of five persons, I carried seven. I decided to take them to their destination in the next village and then return for the evening service. I bought some petrol at the very station I saw in my dream, and I prayed again. About a mile down the road, I heard a loud noise under the car, and the vehicle started running off the road.

The passengers shouted for their lives. I called, *"Jesus!"*, and all of a sudden, someone took the steering wheel from my hand, drove the car and parked it off the main highway onto a bridge, which was without sidewalls. We were just inches from falling into a river, but we were saved. **Is God not good?** We all came out of the car but no one was hurt. I left the car and went back to the evening service. **God is good.**

ATTACKED FOR REVENGE

I went to support a friend who was the main speaker at a Full Gospel Meeting. During the time of ministration (prayer for the sick and people with other needs), a lady with a swollen leg who could not walk was brought for prayers. She felt the power of God as we prayed with her. The Lord laid it on my heart to put my handkerchief on the swollen leg. First, I disobeyed because I thought it would look like spiritual showmanship, but the Holy Spirit reminded me of the handkerchief and I laid it on her leg. She got up, and started walking, jumping and praising God. The crowd joined her in the jubilation.

At the end of the meeting, she said she wanted to share a short testimony. She said about a couple of years back, she had a dream in which she was bitten by a snake. The pain from the dream came to the physical and her leg got swollen so much that she became paralysed. They took her to hospitals but she received no cure. She was taken to the Republic of Togo and to the Republic of Benin, all in West Africa, to witch doctors. But the problem could not be solved. However, on that day, she met Jesus and she was healed.

I returned to my station (Akim Oda) and that very night, I had a dream. In the dream, I saw a green snake, which was about to attack me. I said, *"What shall I use to kill this snake?"* Suddenly, a fenced garden appeared close to me and I saw a rod in it. I lifted up the rod and started walking towards the snake but I saw it disappear into the horizon. I woke up and prayed, and asked God why I could not kill the snake. The Lord answered me thus:

"The battle is not yours. The battle is for the Lord. You cannot kill the devil; you can only submit to God and resist the devil and he will flee from you. That was the snake you casted out of the woman at the meeting. It came here for revenge. I have given you a weapon of resistance. You cannot kill the devil; you can only resist him and he will flee from you."

I thanked the Lord for fighting the battle for me.

ATTACKED BY A WHITE LADY, A PIG AND A COBRA

Spiritual warfare, in many regards, is like normal warfare, but it goes further than normal warfare because you do not see your enemy. There are times to launch offensive weapons, times to hold on to your ground, and times of tactical retreat. There are times for man-to-man combat.

During a deliverance meeting, the Lord delivered about thirty people from spiritual marriages in a night. This happened in Berekum, Brong Ahafo Region, in Ghana. That very night, I was resting in bed when I felt that a naked lady with long hair was in bed with me. I switched on the light and behold, there was a white lady. I shouted the name of Jesus Christ and she disappeared immediately. In the same town, a pig wanted to rape me in a dream and the Lord drove it away. So I prayed a short prayer:

"Lord, I need your protection; if not, I am quitting this job."

As I fell asleep again, I dreamt that I was preaching in a large church and an angry cobra was coming to attack me in the pulpit; but I heard a gunshot, which shattered the cobra. I woke up and praised the Lord. Since then, I have had my peace. Remember that the devil will always attack you to quit the Christian race but, brothers and sisters, I entreat you not to quit.

ATTACKED BY A PRINCIPALITY

As an evangelist, I always travel around ministering. Usually, I ask God to reveal the prince ruling the town or the geographical area to me. Anytime I went to minister, I would bind the prince ruling the geographical zone. This I do under the direction of the Holy Spirit. One day, the Samreboi Chapter of the FGBMFI invited me for a programme. When I got to the town, I did not ask the Lord for the principality in charge of the area. As I started ministering, I felt the spiritual atmosphere very heavy. I felt that nothing happened, but wonderful testimonies came from people.

Back in my guesthouse, I decided to pray all night and ask God for fresh anointing. While praying on my knees, I had a vision in which a big chimpanzee tried to attack me. Then I saw also that the executive members of the FGBMFI were sitting at the high table and merely watching me struggling with the chimpanzee. I asked them, *"Why can't you stop this animal from strangling me?"*

Then a voice answered me, *"Man cannot deliver you."* Then I shouted *"Jesus!"'* and the animal fell on its knees. Two swords came down from above and thrust through its eyes. The following day, it was a miracle harvest: A young man with epilepsy was completely delivered. An illiterate woman, an Ewe, was taught to read the Twi Bible by God. She still reads to this day. Many people were saved. A student of Asankragwa Secondary School who had a spinal cord problem for many years as a result of a motor accident, fell under the power of the Holy Spirit and in a vision, he found himself in a theatre where he underwent surgery. When he got up, the Lord had healed him.

ANOTHER PRINCIPALITY DEFEATED

Believe it or not, it happened in a town called Asankragwa, in the Western Region of Ghana. I was invited to hold an indoor crusade for the core group of the

FGBMFI. While praying for the programme, I saw in a vision a small short snake moving fast in fear. It climbed a tall tree but as it reached the top, a big snake of about five feet long fell from the top of the tree and collapsed. I asked the Lord for the meaning and he told me that the principality ruling the town was the snake.

The following morning, I went to Asankragwa Secondary School to visit the young man whose spinal cord was healed. I told him that the principality of the area had fallen so there would be a miracle harvest in the town. By three o'clock in the afternoon of the same day, the students brought us news that a snake about eight feet in length fell from the top of one of the tallest trees on the campus and collapsed. They killed it and put it into a jar of chemical for preservation in their science laboratory. The devil was in trouble.

At the crusade that night, we had just started singing praises when the power of God moved through the town hall and a cripple was healed. A lady possessed with an evil spirit that called itself "Gabriel" was instantly delivered. Many people gave their lives to Jesus Christ. Thank God, today, there is a chapter of FGBMFI in the town.

God made man in his own image. I believe it is the spiritual image and not the physical image and Jesus said those who believe in Him would do the works He did and even do greater things because He has gone to the Father.

MIRACLES IN THE LIVES OF OTHERS

A NEW BABY

A man invited me to go and pray with his sick wife in the hospital. She had suffered a miscarriage and the doctor had to wash/clean the womb because tests showed that there was no baby in the womb as a result of the bleeding. When I got there, I prayed thus:

"Thank you, Jesus Christ. Now, Satan and you spirits of miscarriage, listen to me; I command you in the name of Jesus Christ to leave this woman and go out through the window because you are thieves. You only come to steal, to kill and to destroy. Holy Spirit, my Comforter and Helper, I humbly request you to send forth an angel doctor from heaven with a new baby for this woman's womb, because of the faith of the husband in you, Jesus Christ. Amen."

The man asked me if that was the whole prayer, and I said yes. Later, when the woman was to be taken to the theatre for the womb to be washed, the Holy Spirit prompted them to test the woman again. The test revealed that there was a baby in the womb. She gave birth to a baby boy later. Yes, a baby was sent from heaven. The man praised the Lord. Everyone marvelled. *Is God not great?* God is indeed great and helpful. He has done it for others, and He will do it for you too.

JESUS HEALED AN AUDITOR

A medical officer invited me to pray for a friend of his, an auditor, who had been ill for months. He had severe pain in one of his legs. He could only hop on one leg and could not go to work for some months. We rode in the doctor's car to the residence of the sick man, who had to hop from his bedroom to the living room to meet us. These were my exact words to him:

"Daddy in the name of Jesus Christ, you will walk on both legs, and will see us off to the car, if you only believe in Jesus. If my God does not heal you, I will go and hand my Bible over to the nearest pastor and quit.".

"Do you believe?" I asked. The man who was in very severe pain said, *"Yes, I do believe."* I was sensitive to the Holy Spirit and this may sound strange to some people but the Lord told me to:

1. Bind all unclean spirits and command them to leave in Jesus Name. (During the process, I got to know that the man was attending an occultist church.)
2. Command the spirit of pain to leave the man. (I did that.)
3. Tell the man to stretch out the painful leg in Jesus Name. (I told him and he stretched out the leg. The pain left the leg immediately.)

4. The Holy Spirit said, *"Pray in the spirit and let him follow you."*

He walked on the two legs without pain. He said, *"Doctor, the pain is gone. I am healed."* He accompanied us to the car and gave his life to Christ. The following Saturday, he attended the Full Gospel Businessmen's Fellowship meeting. He is still well. Praise God. He was immediately promoted and transferred as a regional auditor.

A COLLEAGUE DELIVERED FROM CIGARETTE ADDICTION

A colleague teacher, who was addicted to smoking, confessed that the cost of smoking cigarettes each month exceeded his salary. He was such a nice gentleman and I had a burden for his soul.

One day, the Lord laid it on my heart to fast and intercede for him. I fasted for five days without telling him. One Friday night, around 9pm, I went to his apartment and said to him, *"Mr. Berko, you have stopped smoking"*. He replied, *"Bro. Leo, you are funny. Do you know how long I have been smoking? It is impossible for me to stop."* I told him that I was sent by Jesus Christ and that to God, nothing is impossible. I left him by 10pm.

Saturday morning, as I was interceding for him on my knees, I heard a knock on my door with a loud shout for joy. *"Brother Leo, I have stopped smoking."* When I opened the door, it was Mr. Berko. *"Don't come to tease me this morning,"* I told him. But he replied, *"Brother Leo, this morning, I took my first stick of cigarette and as I was about to smoke, I felt something came out of me and the cigarette fell from my hand. I lost the desire for cigarettes immediately."*

He stopped smoking from that morning and got saved. Since he was the life patron of smokers on the teaching staff, some of the smokers accused me of using the power of Beelzebub the prince of demons, to deliver their patron. Praise the Lord.

A FEMALE STUDENT HEALED

One of my female students had a spiritual problem. Whenever it was getting to the examination period, she would fall sick (and would not be able to read) until the exams would be over. One day, I prayed with her, and while praying, I noticed that she stamped the ground with both feet. When I enquired about why she did that, she told me a snake fell from her body and she crushed it with the soles of her shoes.

When we finished praying, I gave her a Bible to read and she read it fluently. She never felt sick again until she ended her course. She is now working abroad. *Thanks be to God.*

In a particular town, an illiterate lady, an Ewe by tribe, started reading the Holy Bible in a different tribal language: Akuapim Twi. This happened just a night after our crusade. A Muslim was also healed in the name of Jesus. His doctors had advised him not to play lawn tennis because of chest problems. After his healing, he went back to playing tennis.

Sometimes I would pray to God to reveal the principality ruling the area that I visited. After I had bound it in prayers, revival would break out.

A MUSLIM LADY DELIVERED

Among the people delivered in the same town was a Muslim lady. The lady had been sick for a long time and she looked sad and sullen. I could discern from her story that it was a case of spiritual marriage since it was impossible to wake her up when she slept, unless she returned from the spiritual world where her spiritual husband took her every night.

According to the friend who brought her to the church, she had been taken to many mallams without success. We prayed for her and broke the spiritual marriage bondage. After her deliverance, she recounted some of her experiences to us. A Mallam once gave her a type of concoction to drink but the spiritual husband who was a white man covered her mouth with his hand. This prevented the medicine from entering her mouth and it poured on the floor. She saw the spirit, and felt his hand but no one else saw him.

She said that on another occasion when she fell sick, the spirit took her to the Holy Family Hospital in the town and gave her some medicine to take. She took the drugs and became well. She had a child with her boyfriend but the spirit killed the child. The spirit confessed to her that he killed her son. She gave birth to five spiritual babies for the spirit in the spiritual world. The pretty lady, fair in complexion could not have any male partner because according to her, any man who took her for a friend was severely beaten in the night by the spirit.

Immediately after her deliverance, the spirit came to take her away. She told the spirit that Jesus Christ had dissolved the marriage, but the spirit left and came with a spear to kill her. She then called the name of Jesus Christ and the spear was destroyed. Then a fight broke out between them but God empowered her so she pushed the spirit into a bottomless pit. He struggled to come out but to no avail. The lady was baptised into the Holy Spirit and she changed her name to a Christian one. This annoyed the Muslim family and they threatened to kill her. Later on, she left the town for her life's sake. She became part of our ministry where she shared her testimony. We thank God for her life. Thank God I have good Muslim friends.

A PASTOR'S DAUGHTER DELIVERED FROM WITCHCRAFT

While holding a weeklong revival with the Full Gospel Businessmen's Fellowship International, a district pastor of a church visited the meeting. He came for counselling as to the need for Holy Spirit baptism and speaking in tongues. He was a district pastor of Deeper Life church. He and his family lived a pious life. They studied the Word; they knew the Word but did not believe in speaking in tongues and miracles.

After counselling, he was immediately baptized in the Holy Spirit with speaking in tongues. His life changed; his understanding of the Word changed, and he had been anointed to deal with a chronic problem in his family. On my next visit to the town, the pastor came again and told me that his daughter, aged seventeen, confessed to being a witch. He said that for some years the girl was very stubborn and immoral; their money also always disappeared. I told him to bring the girl and she came for counselling. During the deliverance service she vomited some herbs and some objects. She was baptized into the Holy Spirit and committed herself to Jesus Christ.

Her Testimony

She said that one night, her grandmother flew into their house from a town far away and brought her a lot of meat to eat. The grandmother warned her not to tell her parents that she had been there. The following night, she came again and the girl turned into a bird and together they flew away to attend a witches' meeting. Since then, they had been attending witch meetings together.

She had been stealing her father's money with the spirit. One time, she turned into a snake and bit her brother. She herself carried her brother on her back to a clinic since there was no car that night. She later healed him spiritually. She had broken many people's marriages, and rendered men who cheated on her sexually impotent. After the deliverance, the Lord restored the family's finances and farm produce. The father handed her to me and she was with our crusade team for some time.

It was through her testimony that a thirteen-year-old witch surrendered to Christ and was delivered (testimony given in *"Delivered from Voodoo & Witchcraft by Christ"*). She (the 13 year old witch) even attended the world convention of witches in India.

A LADY DELIVERED FROM THE POWER OF DWARFS

While I was ministering in a town, I had a message that a 22-year old lady was taken by dwarfs for five years. They needed someone to help deliver her. She was a student in a secondary school so this affected her education. Like the story in *Acts 16:16,* her parents wanted to make money out of her. The dwarfs gave her magical powers by which she could cut open her abdomen with a sharp razor blade, remove her intestines into a plate and cut them into pieces. She would pull out her tongue and cut it into pieces. She would later put them back intact. I told the young man who brought the message to me that the Lord would deal with the devil when I returned to Kumasi.

One day, however, I was teaching in the FGBMFI meeting at the Kumasi Cultural Centre when the lady was brought dripping in fresh blood. She had just performed the devil's feat again with a crowd following her. I had a relationship with dwarfs when I was a Satanist. We sang for them and worshiped them, and sent them on errands, either to bring information, or steal money. One thing about worshippers of dwarfs is that when they are bound with ropes, they would be freed by the spirits. Knowing this, I spoke to the spirits and said,

"You dwarfs, I know that you cannot be bound by rope but today, I will bind you in the name of Jesus Christ."

As soon as I mentioned Jesus Christ, the spirit started manifesting as a fetish priestess. I commanded the dwarfs to leave in the name of Jesus Christ. They left immediately and the devil could no longer perform his feat through the girl. She accepted Jesus Christ and was later baptized into the Holy Spirit, but her parents got angry and collected all her clothes from her. A Christian brother, however, donated money for new clothes for the girl.

I shall not say much about her testimony, which could seriously bring a church into disrepute. The priest of the church, which failed to deliver her for five years, demanded to have a sexual relationship with her after her deliverance from the dwarfs. The priest of the church told her one needed to have sex after deliverance in order to retain the deliverance. But she refused, and came and reported the case to me. This is a priest of one of the oldest mainline churches. *O God!* He is a priest of a good church. *Are we safe? God, Help your children.*

The girl however refused and told the priest that she wanted to live a holy life. This is how she retained her deliverance. The parents of this lady took her to a popular shrine in the Eastern Region of Ghana for rituals to be performed, so that she could be possessed again, but after the rituals, the girl never got possessed. Thanks be to God.

THE YOUNG WITCHES IN PRESTEA

At a meeting in Prestea, in the Western Region of Ghana, a woman hinted to me that her two daughters were witches so she had brought them for deliverance. They were seven and nine years old, and after deliverance, they shared their experience in the witchcraft world with us.

The Testimony of the Youngest

She told us some of the atrocities they had committed.

1. They took bags of cement from a cement factory, using articulated trucks, and put them under their father's cocoa plantation. This made the farm look very green but it yielded no fruit.
2. They reserved a few trees, which yielded fruit, but they turned into squirrels and ate the fruits.
3. Their father learnt of their nefarious activities from a sorcerer, so he watched the few trees that bore fruit with a gun to kill the squirrels. They knew of all his plans through their powers.
4. They had killed their three-year-old sister. They donated her at the meeting of witches.
5. Their witchcraft pot was jointly owned with other witches; the custodian of the pot was a

Women's Fellowship leader of an orthodox
church in the town.

Their mother said any time she became pregnant, at the
end of the third month, she would dream that a goat
passed between her legs and the following day she
suffered miscarriage. The children claimed responsibility
for the plight of their mother. The woman, who claimed to
be a Christian, could not understand why her two small
children would deal with her and their father like that. She
had forgotten that the spiritual battle is not in age or how
long you have been a Christian. The victory depends on
our commitment to God. I counselled the lady and advised
her to continue staying in the Lord and to desire power
from above.

A SHOP CLOSED ABROAD FOR SELLING ROYAL PYTHONS

I was a guest to some churches abroad. My host decided to
take me for sightseeing in a mall (shopping centre) and as
we went around, we came to a shop that offered pets,
including pythons, for sale. The scripture says God has put
enmity between man and the serpent. I did not see why
people should provide comfortable environment for
snakes and feed them. To my surprise, almost all the
snakes were the types that are worshipped as gods among
my ethnic group. It is a taboo to kill these snakes.

I was angry, so I told my host that I would close down
the shop with prayers but he did not believe it. Two weeks
later, we went to the shopping centre and that particular
shop was closed. It had gone bankrupt because no one was
buying from it. That is what God can do.

HEALING IN AN ASSEMBLIES OF GOD CHURCH, FLORIDA-USA

The scripture says, *"The just shall live by faith"*

It was a good service, which we enjoyed that Sunday morning. The pastor who hosted me the previous year had resigned. My new host was a pastor who also loved me. We were having a chat after service when an old lady came to us, rejoicing in the Lord. She said,

"Pastor, I am grateful to God for healing me last year, when Bro. Leo ministered in our church. Doctors had already given up on me and had given me a few days to live. After the sermon, he invited us for a ministration. He told us to ask God to heal us, and I did so in faith. The Lord healed me. For fourteen months, I have had no medication, yet I am alive and healthy." Praise God. He is good.

LONDON: A YOUNG LAWYER DELIVERED

On my way to Israel for a pilgrimage, I made a stopover in the United Kingdom and was privileged to be a guest speaker at a conference of ministers from all over the world, in Edmonton Temple. At one of the meetings, a young man accompanied by two women walked into the hall while I was preaching. Someone went and whispered into the ears of the host pastor. The pastor interrupted my message to tell me the mission of the young man and the two ladies.

The Challenge

The young man had visited his brother, who witnessed to him about Jesus Christ. He told the two ladies that he had come to the conclusion that Christians have no power, and that they only talk. The ladies then informed him that there was a Satanist who had become a Christian, and now an evangelist, preaching around and asked him whether he would like to test the power of God with the evangelist. The man agreed to test the power of God.

This was the reason for their coming to the church. He stood in front of me with the pride of the devil. I simply told him that I had also had power from the devil before, and that I could see my power had been more than ten times his power. However, now that I have the power of Jesus, I have the greatest power. I then called four men who could pray in the spirit to come and lay hands on him and pray in strange tongues to confuse the devil.

The young lawyer started to sweat profusely, and he began to manifest. After some manifestations, I rebuked the devil in him to leave, and he was delivered. The man had an idol made of cloth in the form of a human figure, which guarded him. This god was always under the seat of his car, but after the prayers, when he got back to his car, he saw that half of the god had been burnt under his car seat. Fire from heaven had burnt it.

The following day, he brought his gods in a carrier bag for me to be burnt. He told me that in the night, he felt as if brimstones of fire were falling down on him and that was why he brought the rest of the gods for burning. He became born again and became filled with the Holy Spirit. It is in prayer that he remains in the faith.

His Story

He told us that before leaving his home country of Nigeria to study law in the UK, his father gave him witchcraft power. Once in a while, he flew with witchcraft power from the UK to West Africa in the night to attend witch meetings with his father. When his girlfriend became pregnant, he did not want the baby so he went to the cemetery, called the child in the spirit and killed the child. Three days later, his girlfriend miscarried. This happened about two weeks before our encounter.

COUNTERFEIT GIFTS IN THE CHURCH

As I explained in my book "Delivered from Voodoo & Witchcraft by Christ", counterfeit gifts operate in the devil's kingdom. I was there and partook in the worship services. It is not hearsay. Gifts of prophecy, vision, strange tongues, healing and miracles operate in voodoo shrines. I have been to places and seen some of these counterfeit gifts operate in churches.

I believe in the gifts of the Holy Spirit. I am a Pentecostal and Charismatic believer. I am baptized into the Holy Spirit and used by God, but I say we should watch and test all spirits and see which is from God and which is from the devil. Let me share two out of the lot of experiences I have had.

CASE 1. During a week-long revival meeting in a large church, the pastor requested to have a retreat for his prayer team to help them to be baptized by Jesus Christ into the Holy Spirit. I had a meeting with them and during the meeting, I had a word of knowledge that the prophetess had a wrong spirit.

She was not only a prominent prayer warrior, she was

also accredited by the church for her gifts of vision, healing and deliverance. In fact, she had a prayer camp in her house where consultations were made and prayers were offered for people. She even sat on platforms with ordained ministers as a prophetess. The Lord told me that the spirit using the woman was not from Him. I prayed a short prayer with her, and then told her to ask God to reveal the source of her gifts.

Early in the morning, she came and said that in the night, she saw that snakes had made a circle, and she was at the centre of it. She was performing miracles. She needed deliverance and the Lord delivered her.

CASE 2. I was at a Christian meeting when a woman was about to give a prophecy. The Holy Spirit told to me to go and stop the spirit prophesying because it was not from God. I went to the woman and commanded the spirit to stop using her and she fell under the power of the Holy Spirit. God delivered her.

Prior to her deliverance, she had been giving prophecies right from the time she was a student in Secondary School to the Teacher Training College, even until she got married. She had been giving prophecies in regional US camp meetings. All this went on, even though her husband was a deliverance team leader. The following year, when I went to Assemblies of God for a programme in this same town, they visited the church and gave me a love offering to thank the Lord. She confessed that she knew there had been a false spirit in her.

CHAPTER 3
DO NOT SEEK HELP FROM SMALL GODS

Normally, out of ignorance, people in times of trouble and need, seek help from shrines, occult centres, spiritualists and false prophets. People also join secret societies and fellowships in the quest for power. But the Bible says that we must look at Jesus because even wise men sought after Him. When one seeks help from evil spirits, one puts a curse on the family for generations.

A COUPLE SOUGHT HELP FROM A GOD OF FERTILITY

A woman brought three abnormal children to me for deliverance. The children were both mentally and physically abnormal. According to the woman, after many years of marriage without children, they sought help from a god. The god blessed them with three children all of whom behaved like mad people. They were all mentally retarded. According to the woman, she wished they had remained childless. The unfortunate thing was that every year, they had to go and pay homage to the gods.

WEALTH FROM THE DEVIL

A man who got wealth from the devil had not been happy for some time. Every year, one of his vehicles was involved in a fatal accident, killing a lot of people. The storey building that he put up had become a haunted house. However, the man was not prepared to repent for fear of losing his wealth and life.

Most of the time, if a person signs a covenant with the spirits and makes a vow, breaking this vow leads to loss of property, insanity and sickness or death. This is only avoided by becoming a real Christian.

MAN DELIVERED OF A SUGAR MUMMY "SCHOLARSHIP" DEMON

A young man heard of my testimony in a camp meeting and confided in me that when he was a student, he had a "scholarship" from a wealthy businesswoman. As a student, it was a jackpot he had hit. He and the lady had a good sexual relationship. One day at dawn, while sleeping with the woman, he felt something cold between him and his darling on the bed. The young man said when he got up to examine the cold touch, he saw a huge snake on the bed. The woman was still sleeping so he ran naked to the living room. He wondered whether it was a dream or a reality, so he went back to the bedroom.

There, to his surprise, he saw the snake entering into the woman through her female organ, as she writhed in pain. He stood and watched everything to the end. When the woman opened her eyes and saw him, she warned him not to tell anybody and gave him a large sum of money. Eventually, he and the woman broke up. But since then, his life was miserable. He became poor and had no job. He went outside the country and came back without anything. I prayed with him and he was delivered. After his deliverance, he got a job, with a company car at his disposal.

This story did not surprise me because many women who seek power to have flourishing businesses end up with spiritual snakes in their bellies. These snakes are fed by men who sleep with these women because the snakes feed on the sperm of the men they sleep with.

There was another lady who fell sick and almost died because while she was a maidservant to a businesswoman in Togo, she entered her madam's room unannounced. She saw a snake vomiting money. The girl went dumb for almost a year and the relatives had to take her for deliverance. By the grace of God, she is fine today. She does not want to talk for fear of a spiritual attack.

MY FRIEND WANTED THE DEVIL'S MONEY

Once I met my father's friend, an elderly man in Takoradi. He invited me to his house where I met his son, who was my friend. In a conversation, the son told me that he called spirits and practised both black and white magic. He told me of his adventures in the spiritual world. One of the spirits would steal money from people, companies and banks in large quantities and show it to my friend. However, he was not permitted to spend the money. The spirits would take the money back.

Eventually, my friend, who was then unemployed, told me of how he had made up his mind to get rich quickly through the help of a witch doctor. The witch doctor asked him whether he has the heart for money, and he had answered yes. My friend bought all the items for the ritual and went to the shrine for the ceremony. He had big dreams of a large house, a new car, etc. He had gone through the various stages of the ritual until the final stage when a calabash of water was placed before him with the image of his father, his spouse and their newly born baby in it. He was given a dagger to stab the images and the water would turn into blood. The people would die and money would not be his problem.

As he held the dagger in his hand and looked at his father, the breadwinner of the family, his lady and the baby, he started sweating and shivering. He thought the devil would accept a poor man. He excused himself from the witchdoctor to go and urinate, and ran away. It was divine intervention that saved his relatives.

The fact was his father was a Christian. He cared for their extended family, but he did not have a personal relationship with Jesus Christ. He did not have any authority as a believer. **Someone might decide to use you also in exchange for money, and you may not be aware. Why not take insurance cover under Jesus Christ and become born again?**

A BUSINESS DELIVERED

Deut. 8:18 *says, "And you shall remember the Lord your God, for it is He who gives you power to get wealth, that He may establish His covenant which He swore to your fathers as it is in this day."*

The Lord is the one who gives us strength to acquire wealth, in order to expand His kingdom. It is good for Christians to do genuine business and become very rich. But when this happens, we should not forget God. Some businesses fail due to poor management, no matter how prayerful the director and the staff might be. In such cases we do not blame the devil. In other cases, Satan simply attacks the business in order to frustrate the work of the kingdom. There are many reasons for the failure of companies but I would like to take a look at an example.

I met a woman in the transport business on one of my revival meetings, and she told me she needed deliverance from a witchcraft spirit. She told me that her sister gave her the spirit. She said she and her sister operated in the spiritual realm by taking a minibus from their village in Ghana and travelling to Liberia to bring in goods. They would return the same night. One day on their return, they were late so they forgot a headgear (headscarf) and a cloth in the bus.

The following morning, the driver was surprised and wondered at how these things were left in the bus, which was washed and locked up the previous evening. The tyres showed that the vehicle had been used in the night. Since it was a small village, they were able to identify the owners of the items as belonging to her sister and another woman. They were confronted and asked to explain how the bus became dusty, with their headgear and cloth left inside.

They confessed that they were witches and that they used the bus in the spirit and it manifested in the physical. The Lord delivered this lady who came to see me. *Thank God for Jesus Christ.*

MIRACLE CHILDREN

The Lord has blessed many families with children through our ministry. Some of these children are named after me.

In London, many women were also blessed with children. In a church at Tesano, Accra, the Lord used the ministry to provide children to childless couples.

In one town, a woman whose womb was removed spiritually and tied to a cloth by the mother for five years, was healed. After praying with her, she had a dream that a man was beating her mother. The mother pleaded with her daughter to tell the man to stop beating her. That very month, the lady became pregnant. Her mother confessed to being a witch and had taken her daughter's womb for all the past years. The lady delivered, through surgery, a baby girl named Gifty.

The Lord continues to bless us with signs and wonders. The problem with Christians is that they chase miracles more than knowing the Word so any one who claims to have miraculous power becomes a god. I believe that every Christian must study the Word and be able to stand on his spiritual feet.

People asked Jesus for more signs but He did not give it to them; rather, he taught them. No wonder He was called Rabbi in the Bible, which means Teacher. We need miracles to balance our ministry in these end times. The signs should follow believers and not believers following signs. You are a vessel of signs and wonders, if only you will study the Word and live the Word with faith in God.

THE STORY OF AN EX-FETISH PRIEST

This former fetish priest was one of my testimony team members. He was asked to join my team and be trained to grow in the ways of the Lord. He was saved at a crusade of another former fetish priest. After going through a series of deliverance sessions, he accompanied us on our mission field. He was baptised into the Holy Spirit by Jesus.

His Testimony

One day, he went to the riverside to fetch some water. When he got to the bank of the river, he heard someone call him, and he replied, thinking it was one of his friends. He left his bucket and followed the direction of the call. He mysteriously entered a new world of dwarfs. They were short beings in stature, very old looking with long beards. Their feet pointed backwards (i.e. from the opposite direction of normal human feet). Apart from this abnormality and their very short stature, they looked like human beings.

As a stranger, they crowded around to examine him. They showed him some hospitality. After the meeting, they took his clothing from him and removed his sandals. They replaced his clothing with a small smock to fit him. They changed his hair into "Rasta" (dreadlocks) style with cowries and small bells attached. They gave him spiritual regalia. He stayed with them for three days, and whenever he was hungry, the dwarfs ate bananas and rubbed their hands on his mouth. This kept him satisfied without eating for three days.

On the third day, in the evening, they asked him for his favourite meal. He said fufu and light soup. Immediately, fufu and hot light soup in an earthenware bowl was before him, with a lot of fish and meat in the soup. They asked him to eat it because they would bring him home that evening. He enjoyed the meal. During this time, a search party had been organized by the village for him.

After the meal, they took him to the bank of the river.

When the women who had gone to fetch water saw him, they argued among themselves. Some said it was the young man who was missing; others said the person they saw was a madman with long dirty hair with cowries and bells, and just in pants (trousers). He decided to follow the women. When they got to the village, the elders recognised him and they knew that he had been taken by dwarfs and made a fetish priest.

They performed the rites, got him a stool and prepared him as a priest. All this time, he could not speak. According to him, around mid-night, a dwarf came into his room, carried him on his shoulder to the forest and asked him to command a big tree to wither. He shouted and the tree dwindled into ashes. The dwarfs told him that from that time he could speak to people. If he had first spoken to a human being, the person would have died, except if the person was a committed Christian.

Now as a priest of the devil, the young man started performing miracles for the devil. He would pluck a leaf and it would change into a bank note (paper money). He got the gifts of sorcery, divination, and others from the devil. He had been able to use the power to cast spells on many women and had intimacy with them. Businesswomen trooped into his shrine for help. These included some churchgoers.

A man sought his assistance to open a spiritual church that would draw the wealthy in the society. After bargaining, the prospective pastor was to pay a token fee as the church grew. He was to pay this sum of money regularly for thanksgiving to the shrine. The deal was closed and the church started. The founder and pastor operated very well in miracles of healing and prosperity for clients and members alike. The church had a large congregation. One day, the pastor refused to keep paying the token fee to him. The dwarfs, consequently, killed the pastor and his elders, one after the other. The church later collapsed.

As I said earlier, this young man had been with my testimony team. We visited Dormaa-Ahenkro, Sunyani and some towns in Ghana. *When one leaves the devil's camp, one needs the Word, prayer and fasting and a committed Christian life to survive.* During our Dormaa crusade, I was lodging in the Presbyterian Church of Ghana Mission House. My team was lodging at a hotel opposite Dormaa-Ahenkro hospital, belonging to one Mr. Nkrumah.

One night after our meeting, I met the young man, who was supposed to be either praying or sleeping, in town at about 11:30pm. He was in the company of some worldly boys and I told him to return to the hotel and sleep. I then drove the other boys away. By one o'clock in the morning, the other team members ran to my place to report that the former priest had been sent to the hospital.

According to them, when the young man returned from town, they were praying, and after the prayers, they slept. Not long afterwards, they heard the young man screaming for help. They went to him and he told them he was enjoying fresh air in front of the hotel around midnight, when a cobra came and spat into his eyes and disappeared.

In the hospital, the nurses quickly washed his eyes and called the doctor. The eyes were examined and by God's grace, no wound had developed in them. He was treated and discharged.

From Dormaa-Ahenkro, we went to the Assemblies of God Church in Sunyani for a revival. At the end of the revival, the ex-fetish priest lied to us, saying he wanted to go and give a friend's camera to him. I granted him permission to go but he never returned.

Later on, his colleagues told me that he said he would not come back because there is no money in God's work. He told them of how when he was in the devil's shrine, he started building a mansion, which got to the window level in a short time. We keep praying for him. We later learnt that he went back to look for the dwarfs to give him power but they made him mad (insane) instead. I know the Lord would heal him one day.

MENTAL CASES HEALED

We cannot understand God and we cannot counsel Him. Sometimes, you see God heal some people miraculously; sometimes, he does not. The scripture says our ways are not His ways. Many mental cases were healed by God in our ministry. I would like to share one or two with you.

I was holding a revival meeting at a church in Kumasi when they brought a lady who was mentally sick. The power of God touched her and she was later taken home. According to her parents, when they got home, she vomited that evening and her sanity returned.

Mental Patient Healed in London

I was in Obuasi (in Kumasi) when a woman approached me that her sister in London was suffering from a mental disorder and that the doctors were not able to cure her. I interceded for three days with fasting and prayers. On the third day, I saw in a dream that a woman was phoning from London to tell me that she was well. The following week, the family sent some family members to bring her down to Ghana for treatment, only to learn that the exact day I had the dream, she was healed. She woke up and the problem had disappeared.

A Chained-Up Mad Woman Healed

I worked as a Healing and Deliverance Evangelist with Calvary Charismatic Centre in Kumasi. I trained men and women in the ministry of God and God has used that ministry mightily. During one of our deliverance services, a mad woman with a chain and a big padlock on her feet ran to the church. She had escaped from a healing camp of a church in Buokrom. She had walked for about three miles to our church. No one led her to us but God.

The camp attendants used a taxi cab to chase her to our church to ask if we had seen a woman in chains. We said yes, but she was in the temple listening to the Word of God. They wanted to take her away by forceful means but she threatened that if they did, she would destroy them together with the taxi cab. We had to calm down the men and promise that we would bring her to their camp at the end of the service.

The Lord instantly healed this woman to the surprise of everyone and she sang to praise the Lord. At the end of the service, she was completely sane. We took her back to the camp in my car, but the camp leader was furious and commanded that the lady be chained up like an animal while her illiterate mother had nothing to say. So she was chained again. But when we were leaving, she called me to pray with her again. It was rather sad.

The next Sunday, the woman was neatly dressed and came to worship with us. She said when we left the camp, they asked her a number of questions and she answered every question intelligently. They were ashamed and released her to go home. She continued attending our services for about a month. God healed her. *Our God is able and is good.*

A MAN WITH DIARRHOEA FOR SIX YEARS HEALED INSTANTLY

I was ministering to the Women Aglow Fellowship International, Obuasi branch, one evening, when a man walked in with a note from a medical officer. The medical officer stated that this man had had diarrhoea for six years and all medications in all the major hospitals in the country could not help him. He had grown very lean so he needed spiritual assistance from God. I simply laid hands on his stomach and felt under my hand as if liquid was being poured from one container into another. I told the congregation that God had healed the man. The following day, the man came and reported that he had been healed. This was on a Tuesday. I asked him to come on Friday, which was the end of the revival, to make sure of his healing. On Friday, he came and told his story.

His Story

In 1986, he ate rice and beans, after which he started visiting the toilet six to twelve times a day. This had gone on for the past six years and as a result, he had been to all the major hospitals in the country. He even spent two years in a Pentecostal Church Prayer Camp (name withheld), all to no avail.

The Obuasi medical officer, who is a Christian, referred him to God. He said that on the first day he was coming to the meeting, he had to control his bowels with much effort. But as soon as I laid my hands on him, he was healed and went to the toilet once a day from then on. A year later, I saw him still healed. He told me his church does not believe in miracles but with his case, they changed their minds.

There are many people bound by denominational spirits. They are bound by spirits of church names. They cannot move out. They cannot change. Some know they are not living as the Word teaches, but the evil spirit makes them give excuses. Some even don't receive any teachings in their churches. Some are in the church but without their Bibles. Some put their Bibles under their pillows when they want to sleep, but that is not Christianity.

Please break away from the denominational spirits. Read the Word and practise what the Word says. Whatever God says to you, just do it. Don't modify it. I am a Christian and also open-minded; please, be critical about scriptural and doctrinal matters. I do what the Bible says and not what man says.

THE BATTLE IS FOR THE LORD

Remember that the battle is for the Lord. The battle is not yours to fight. The only thing is that we must do what God expects of us and the Lord will perform His part.

In other words, what man cannot do, God does; He is the Lord of impossibilities. The problem with mankind today, including myself, is that we are not living a life that is pleasing to God. But we always want to reap the fruits of a holy life. God looks at a man's heart and judges man's motives. He knows our thoughts. I want to tell you that do not allow the devil to occupy your life. Look to God; trust in God. Believe that He will do it.

He fought for Jehoshaphat (*I Chr. 2:20*), He fought for Gideon (*Judges 6:8*), He fought for David (*1 Sam. 16:17*) and many others. He will fight for us also. You need to give your life to Jesus, if you have not yet done so. If you have, then continue your walk with the Lord steadfastly.

PRAYER OF SALVATION

My dear reader, time is running out. If you have never accepted Jesus Christ as your Lord and Personal Saviour, today is your day.

I want you to reflect on your life and find out the answer to this question for yourself: *"Should the world end today by any means, will you go to Heaven or Hell?*

If you want to accept the Lord Jesus as your Lord and Personal Saviour, say the below prayer from your heart.

> *Lord Jesus Christ, I realise that I am a sinner and I cannot save myself. Come into my heart as my Lord and Saviour. Jesus, forgive me my sins. From today, I want to live a holy life unto God. Thank you Jesus Christ. Amen.*

CONCLUSION: Find a good church that believes in the Bible, study the Bible for yourself and fellowship with them.

God bless you.

ABOUT THE AUTHOR

Dr. Leonard Soku, known as Brother Leo, was born into a pagan family in the Volta Region of Ghana in West Africa. While in the womb of his mother and after his birth, he was initiated into demonic cults. Brother Leo was trained by his father at a tender age to succeed him as a voodoo priest, but God had other plans. In November 1986, he had an encounter with Jesus Christ when he attended a Full Gospel Business Men's Fellowship International (FGBMFI) breakfast meeting in Akim Oda, Ghana.

Brother Leo, an Author, a Theologian, a retired Tutor in Accounting, Law and an International Evangelist has written a number of books on his personal life testimony, other teaching materials on spiritual warfare, demonology and curses. He is a gifted healing minister, a conference speaker, and an authority on spiritual warfare. Brother Leo and his wife are lifetime members of Full Gospel Business Men's Fellowship International in Accra, Ghana. They are blessed with two children. Brother Leo is the founder of Radiant Life Christian Centre and Brother Leo Ministries in Accra, Ghana.

ALSO BY DR LEORNARD SOKU

Biblical Fasting & Prayer

Some Useful Hints on Practical Deliverance

Alcohol Consumption Examined from the Scriptures

How to Break Curses

Delivered from Voodoo & Witchcraft by Christ

(Vol. I of "Breaking through the Kingdom of Darkness")

The Spiritual Warfare in the Warzone